The Verbal And Emotional Abuser

Recognizing The Verbal Abusive Relationship And How To Defend Yourself

By

Michele Gilbert

<u>Visit My Amazon Author Page</u>

Dedicated to those who choose to stretch beyond their own limits and to seek a more abundant and fulfilling life.

Your thoughts are creative.

Michele Gilbert

My Free Gift To You!

As a way of saying thank you for downloading my book, I am willing to give you access to a selected group of readers who (every week or so) receive inspiring, life-changing kindle books at deep discounts, and sometimes even absolutely free.

Wouldn't it be great to get amazing Kindle offers delivered directly to your inbox?

Wouldn't it be great to be the first to know when I'm releasing new fresh and above all sharply discounted content?

But why would I so something like this?

Why would I offer my books at such a low price and even give them away for free when they took me countless hours to produce?

Simple…. Because I Want To Spread The Word!

For a few short days Amazon allows Kindle authors to promote their newly released books by offering them deeply discounted (up to 70% price discounts and even for free. This allows us to spread the word extremely quickly allowing users to download thousands and thousands of copies in a very short period of time.

Once the timeframe has passed, these books will revert back to their normal selling price. That's why you will benefit from being the first to know when they can be downloaded for free!

So are you ready to claim your weekly Kindle books?

You are just one click away! Follow the link below and sign up to start receiving awesome content

Thank you and Enjoy!

Table of contents

Introduction

CHAPTER 1: Understanding an Abuser

CHAPTER 2: The Consequences of Abuse

CHAPTER 3: Abuse in an Intimate Relationship

CHAPTER 4: Managing the Pain

Conclusion

Introduction

I want to thank you and congratulate you for downloading this book.

Presented in this book are strategies for understanding and identifying abusive individuals. Being able to understand abusive behavior and identify its first stage, verbal abuse, is the key to freeing yourself from the grasp of an abusive person. By identifying verbal abuse as it occurs, you can possibly avert the chance of verbal abuse escalating into physical abuse. To begin to understand abuse, you must understand why people become abusive. Secondly, you must learn the consequences of abuse. Thirdly, you will learn what forms verbal abuse takes within the bounds of an intimate relationship. And, finally, how to manage and free yourself of the pain caused by an abuser.

So, if you are ready to take the first steps towards freedom from verbal abuse, then let's get started. Gaining knowledge is an empowering experience and can lead to greater personal freedom and self-fulfillment.

Thanks again for downloading this book, I hope you enjoy it!

© Copyright 2015 by Michele Gilbert- All rights reserved.

This document is geared towards providing exact and reliable information in regards to the topic and issue covered. The publication is sold with the idea that the publisher is not required to render accounting, officially permitted, or otherwise, qualified services. If advice is necessary, legal or professional, a practiced individual in the profession should be ordered.

- From a Declaration of Principles which was accepted and approved equally by a Committee of the American Bar Association and a Committee of Publishers and Associations.

In no way is it legal to reproduce, duplicate, or transmit any part of this document in either electronic means or in printed format. Recording of this publication is strictly prohibited and any storage of this document is not allowed unless with written permission from the publisher. All rights reserved.

The information provided herein is stated to be truthful and consistent, in that any liability, in terms of inattention or otherwise, by any usage or abuse of any policies, processes, or directions contained within is the solitary and utter responsibility of the recipient reader. Under no circumstances will any legal responsibility or blame be held against the publisher for any reparation, damages, or monetary loss due to the information herein, either directly or indirectly.

Respective authors own all copyrights not held by the publisher.

The information herein is offered for informational purposes solely, and is universal as so. The presentation of the information is without contract or any type of guarantee assurance.

The trademarks that are used are without any consent, and the publication of the trademark is without permission or backing by the trademark owner. All trademarks and brands within this book are for clarifying purposes only and are the owned by the owners themselves, not affiliated with this document.

CHAPTER 1
Understanding an Abuser

Humans are complicated and complex beings. From the very moment of our birth, we interact with countless other people. How we turn out as unique individuals is a result of numerous unseen factors like genetics and subtle environmental cues. We also are shaped by the social environments in which we grow and mature. Which one of these factors affects our development more is a matter of contention among psychologists and scientists alike. The nature v. nurture argument shows no sign of letting up anytime soon. These essential realities of our identity and how we become who we are cannot be denied.

However, sometimes an individual, for a myriad of reasons, can evolve into an abusive person. It is a well-established fact that many abusive individuals are products of abuse themselves. David M. Allen, M.D. says "While it is important to realize that not all abusers were abused as children, and that many if not most people who are abused do not go on to become abusers themselves, child abuse is most likely the single largest factor - biological, psychological, or sociological - for later adult abusive behavior." In this respect, many abusers are victims of abuse and cannot be judged without keeping that simple fact in mind.

If someone close to you is verbally abusive, then there is a strong likelihood that at some point during their life they experienced physical, verbal, emotional, or sexual abuse. If you are in a position to do so, it might be beneficial to discover more about why the abuser close to you behaves in the manner in which they do. They may be reluctant to open up to you about these experiences, as the experiences have caused them a lot of trauma and pain. If they are open to the possibility, then suggest seeing a therapist. If they are willing to seek professional help, then be supportive in their pursuit to find healing. But if your attempts to understand the abuser close to you are fruitless, and they are unwilling to seek professional help, then the only thing left to understand is how abusers become the abusive individuals they are.

Although abuse during childhood is a common trait of abusive individuals, as mentioned before, it is not present on every case of an abusive individual. However, just because an abuser wasn't abused physically doesn't mean there wasn't any dysfunction in their upbringing. Familial dysfunction can manifest in many various forms. For example, emotional abuse can be very subtle and hard to spot. Furthermore, subtle emotional abuse can sometimes be repressed or difficult to remember. Emotional abuse is not always as obvious as yelling, insulting, or threatening speech. Emotional abuse can take the form of passive-aggressive speech, unhealthy comparisons ("You're not as pretty as your sister" or "If only you were as smart as your brother"), or even emotional neglect.

Abusive manifestations like these, especially passive aggressive speech and emotional neglect, can take their toll on a young child. But they may not have a conscious bearing on their mind. Or, in other words, these abusive behaviors may have been interpreted by the abused as normal behavior. In fact, they may blame themselves for this behavior. This self-blame is true for the physically abused, as well. It is important to understand abuse as a cycle. Abuse is a cycle that often repeats itself. It may change forms or focus, however. For example, an abused child may continue the cycle of abuse during adulthood, but not by abusing another, but by abusing themselves in the form of alcohol or drug abuse and self-harm. Knowing all this, it is possible that even the abuser in your life is willing to talk to you about the abusive experiences in their past, they may not know the full extent of the abuse.

If this is the case, then the best strategy is to try to understand as much as possible about the nature of their upbringing. How was their relationship with their parents? Often, abusive individuals were influenced negatively by the presence of a narcissistic individual. Due to the controlling and emotionally manipulative qualities of a narcissist, children raised by narcissists are sometimes subjected to emotional or physical abuse. However, it is important to note that not every narcissist is physically, or even emotionally, abusive. There are a multitude of personality disorders that a parent or close loved-one might have that could contribute to a child's abusive behavior later in life.

Unfortunately, you don't have to be a narcissist or have a personality disorder to cause damage in a child's life- the kind of damage that goes on to influence their actions as abusers. Neglecting a child emotionally, while not necessarily abusive, can be very detrimental to a child and can contribute to later abusive behavior. So, what is neglect? Well, neglect can be as simple as not acknowledging the child's importance. For the neglectful parent, they can simply not put a priority on the time they spend, if it exists at all, with their children. People who spend more time in the office than with their children can put their children at risk for emotional immaturity. This immaturity can preclude them towards being abuse. However, don't forget that some parents are intentionally neglectful and make it a point to disregard their children's emotional needs. In these cases especially, a child's emotional development can shed light on why they have become abusers themselves.

Without a doubt, an abusers childhood and upbringing have a lot to do with why they behave in an abusive manner. However, childhood abuse is not the only source for an abusive individual's behavior. Drug and alcohol abuse are significant factors, as well. There are also many factors like genetics, hormonal imbalances, or even nutritional deficiencies that can increase aggressive behavior. However, every individual is different. As mentioned elsewhere, each of these common traits of an abusive individual could be present in someone who has never engaged in abusive behavior. All in all, what distinguishes an abuser is their abusive behavior that is directed towards themselves or others.

CHAPTER 2
The Consequences of Abuse

Understanding why someone might behave in an abusive manner is the first step towards liberating yourself from these individuals. If your partner is the abusive individual, then there is an added level of urgency to the matter. However, in situations such as these, it is not merely enough to understand why or how they became abusers. It is equally, if not more important, to understand what happens to ourselves as a recipient of abuse at the hands of our partner or someone close to you.

In the last chapter, you learned that abusive individuals have most likely experienced some form of abuse during the course of their childhood. Logically, it goes without saying that the first and foremost consequence of abuse is the possibility of creating another abusive individual. People who are abused are much more likely to abuse others. Beyond abuse, people who are abused are likely to engage in other negative emotional behavior. Passive-aggressiveness, belittlement, and harsh verbal ridicule are all symptoms of someone's reaction to abuse. Something that must be stressed, however, is that no matter the situation, abusive behavior is a choice. No one is forced to be verbally or physically abusive. That, of course, doesn't mean that the cards haven't been stacked against them, so to speak. Ultimately, we are responsible for our own behavior. Besides continuing a cycle of abuse there are several other consequences of abuse.

What happens to us when we are abused?

When we find ourselves on the receiving end of an abusive relationship, there are several things that can happen to us. Every individual responds to abuse differently. Some individuals will meet abuse with a stern retaliation. Meaning, some people will not tolerate physical or verbal abusive and make that quite clear from the get go. Some will voice their objections, but over time will slowly succumb to allowing the abusive behavior to persist. Others, still, will react to the abuse in a very receptive way, maybe even to the point of seeing the abuse as normal and the abuser's behavior as justified.

But what does this behavior change about us? For those who resist it and do not allow it in their life, perhaps their resolve is strengthened, albeit their faith in humanity somewhat diminished. For those that allow themselves to receive abusive treatment many things begin to change. By allowing the behavior to continue, the abusive individual has no reason to stop. Abuse, whether they are aware of it or not, is a method they use in order to get what they want. This could mean belittling someone else to make themselves feel better, or perhaps verbally threatening someone else in order to intimidate them. In short, being abused invites future abuse.

In fact, our own brains change when we experience regular abuse. We have cells in our brains called synapses. Think of your synapses as the "wiring" in your brain. When we experience anything on a regular basis, our synapses arrange themselves to make the process easier. Think about it. How is it that if you wake up in the middle of the night, you can walk to your kitchen or bathroom half-asleep and in total darkness? Could you do that in someone else's house with the same results? Probably not. This is because you brain has wired itself to be more efficient at completing those processes. And since those processes are regular and repetitive, your brain more or less gets used to them.

When it comes to abuse, this same process is at work. Individuals who are on the receiving end of habitual verbal or physical abuse have undergone changes in their brain. These changes in some way help the individual. In one respect, this process helps to protect the individual form the shock and lesson the blow, so to speak, of the verbal abuse. The body itself becomes used to the abuse in order to protect itself. In short, the brain is enacting its self-protection mode. However, this process has detrimental effects as well. As the brain rewires itself, it makes the stimuli seem more moral, and as your brain gets used to the abuse, so do you. This makes it more difficult to take action and attempt to change the situation.

Our emotional health is another area where the effects of abuse can be seen. Our emotions are very sensitive to abusive behavior. As emotional beings, our interactions are very heavily bound to our emotional makeups and the emotional makeups of others. Of course, as mentioned earlier, every individual reacts differently to abusive behavior. Nevertheless, there are some commonalities among those subjected to abuse.

The most obvious change to one's emotional well-being in the presence of abuse is damage to our self-esteem. This damage can manifest in many ways. Abuse has a way of making the abused question themselves. Abuse can make the abused focus on the negative aspects of their person, while disregarding the positive aspects. The abused may lose interest in activities they once held dear. They may neglect other relationships and become withdrawn. They may exhibit signs of depression. They may even entertain suicidal thoughts or attempt to self-harm. Each of these symptoms should be cause for concern. An injured self-esteem is never beneficial. When our self-esteem is injured or threatened, we become susceptible to further abuse.

Our emotional well-being can be affected greatly by the presence of abuse. There is no way to specifically identify how each individual will respond to abuse. Also, some people will attempt to hide the effects of emotional abuse. There are many reasons for this. The key thing to remember is that no matter if the effects are seen or unseen they are still taking their toll behind the scenes. Needless to say, the results are not beneficial. No one experiences abuse to no effect. Being aware of these possible effects of abuse is the first step towards being free from the negative effects of abuse.

CHAPTER 3
Abuse in an Intimate Relationship

No matter the source, the effects of abuse are often detrimental and should be avoided at all costs. However, sometimes the person who is verbally abusive is an individual who is very close to you. When you are in this situation, you are forced into a very difficult position. Being in this situation is very challenging to anyone who finds themselves trapped between choosing to continue receiving the abuse or to take an active role in avoiding the abuse. When your boss is verbally abusive, you can report their behavior, request a transfer, or, if all else fails, you can always find another job. When a stranger is abusive, you can avoid them. You can't always avoid one-off situations when a passerby says hurtful things, but you can manage the environments and people you associate with. When a close friend is abusive, you can tell them that behavior is unnecessary and unwanted, or even cut your ties with them. But what do you do when your significant other is the one who is abusive? Some people would say you can treat them the same way as anyone else. That is, if someone is abusive, then remove that person from your life. Sometimes, however, it is not always so easy to do.

Obviously, abuse within a relationship is a tell-tale sign that the relationship isn't very healthy. It doesn't take a relationship expert or couple's therapist to see that. When a partner is abusive verbally there may be other issues at play. Infidelity, dishonesty, and even physical abuse are common in relationships where verbal abuse is present. There are a multitude of negative effects that come with a relationship that is marred by verbal abuse. Some of these effects affect us directly. The last chapter focused on how these effects change us personally.

However, let's take into consideration that the effects of verbal abuse can be very subtle. Also, they can not only take a toll on us, but the negative effects of verbal abuse can take their toll on our relationships. With this in mind, let's consider the negative effect abuse has on our relationships.

When our partner exhibits abusive behavior we face a dilemma. On one hand, all abuse is bad and no one should have to endure the pain abuse causes. No one wants to be abused emotionally. Every individual has a strong and innate desire to be loved and accepted by others in our lives. This desire is one of our prime reasons for seeking out a partner in the first place. Without these desires to be loved and accepted, we'd be nothing more than animals who seek reproductive mates. But we do have these desires; we do have an essential part of ourselves that longs to be treated well by those closest to us. However, our need for affection can act like an emotional Achilles heel. Furthermore, this desire can overpower other aspects of our being. Sometimes the desire to be loved can be so strong that we allow ourselves to be treated in ways that hurt our emotional selves, and sometimes even our physical bodies. It may be very difficult to acknowledge that your partner is being abusive. But you need to understand how suffering emotional abuse will affect your relationships, both with your partner and with others.

When our partner abuses us, we lose trust in that individual. Trust is one of the key building blocks of a healthy relationship. This fact is true no matter the type of relationship in question. For example, even business or professional relationships require trust. The closer and more intimate the relationship, then the higher level of trust that is needed. In general, humans need to be secure in the fact that those around us can be trusted. It is both natural and practical to seek assurances that our trust in others is justified. Abusive behavior erodes trust. When we experience abuse, we put our guard up, so to speak. However, when those who are the closest to us begin to exhibit abusive behavior when our defenses are down, the damage that is done by those closest to us does the most damage and causes the most pain.

The first casualty in a relationship is trust. Once trust disappears, only a shell of a relationship remains. It is almost like a building on a Hollywood set. On the outside, it looks like a real building, but on the inside there is no furniture, no appliances, and not even any walls. In short, without trust a relationship is nothing more than a cheap knock off of the real thing. Deep down, it is impossible to trust someone who abuses you. For some people, it is next to impossible to trust people who treat them well and give them no reasons not to be trusted! Think how abuse complicates this.

Besides damaged trust, we begin to doubt ourselves. We begin to doubt our own perception of events. This can have several ramifications. The worst result, by far, is that we can begin to blame ourselves for the abusive behavior. We can begin to rationalize and justify our abusive partner's behavior. In extreme cases, we can begin to believe that we deserve the behavior. At the same time, because we begin to doubt ourselves, we put more and more faith in our partner. We naturally turn to them for emotional shelter. But, since they are the cause of the emotional pain in the first place, we are denied the healing we so desperately seek.

If you ever wonder how individuals endure years and years of physical abuse, yet still do not condemn their partner for their behavior, then know that this is the reason for such perplexing behavior. Sometimes, we can begin to not only sympathize with our abusers, but see ourselves through their own crooked and selfish viewpoints. It is a vicious cycle where the abused seeks to heal the damage done and finds the only person available to offer healing is the abuser. In addition to our fractured trust, the very way we see ourselves and how others treat us is perverted and forced to conform to the point of view of our abuser.

However, abuse or not, we do care about our partners. Our point of view may not be so corrupted as to totally disregard our own feelings and desires. This is the space that you most likely occupy if you are reading this Ebook. You desire a change. You are aware of a problem. By building on your understanding and learning more, you are taking proactive measures. You want both you and your partner to be happy. All you want is just a peaceful and loving relationship. You may wonder, if the verbal abuse can come under control, if then the relationship will be in a better and healthier place.

Beyond trust and how we view ourselves, there are several other things that are immediately affected when it comes to our relationships. As mentioned before, abuse can make us emotionally withdrawn. Just like pulling your hand away from something hot, our mind withdraws itself when faced with painful stimuli. When abused, we lose a lot of our emotional availability. Therefore, making meaningful and lasting connections with other individuals becomes increasingly difficult. This is not only true for our romantic relationships. Because of our painful experiences we may react by neglecting our other relationships. Our close relationships with friends may slowly decay. We may avoid meeting new people, even going out of our way to avoid situations where meeting new people usually occurs. We may slowly withdraw all contact from other individuals including our colleagues, peers, or even our family members.

Furthermore, our ability to communicate our emotions becomes hampered. The concatenation of damaged trust, an unhealthy self-image, and emotional unavailability creates a potent cocktail that hampers our communicative abilities. Due to the combination of all these things, communicating how we feel becomes increasingly difficult. As open and honest communication is another pillar of a healthy relationship, just as important as trust, any relationship we are a part of suffers because of the damage caused by abuse. Think of damaged communication as a metaphorical last nail in the coffin. Because once we get to the point where communication is difficult, if not impossible, we find ourselves in a situation that is difficult to change. Nevertheless, this situation is manageable. You just have to learn how.

CHAPTER 4
Managing the Pain

By now, you've learned to understand the abuser. You've learned some of the major causes of an abusive individual's behavior. You have learned the consequences of abuse and how abuse affects relationships. Now, you will learn some ways of managing the pain cause by an abusive partner. This step in the process is the most important. What you choose to do from this point will have the greatest bearing on the outcome of your relationship. It is simply not enough only to understand; you must take action. Being proactive will ensure that you see real and positive change. It is the first step towards realizing a happy and healthy relationship that is totally free of abuse.

We cannot erase the past. Although cliché, this statement is sobering and true. There is nothing we can do to change what has happened to us. Furthermore, we cannot change our memories. They best thing we can do is to take proactive steps by addressing our memories and trying to move on. In the meantime, however, there are some strategies we can use to mitigate the negative effects of abuse in our lives.

Firstly, we can limit the power our abusers have over us, whether that means reevaluating our relationships, deciding whether or not to pursue a future with our abusers. You can also limit your abuser's power by standing up for yourself and setting boundaries. You can make it clear that that type of behavior is totally unacceptable, and that you will not tolerate that behavior from anyone. This may seem like a daunting, or even impossible, task. However, you must find the courage to stand up for yourself and set some boundaries. Do this by expressing exactly what about your partner's behavior bothers you. What words or phrases anger you? How do the words of your partner make you feel? Make sure your abusive partner is well aware of these things.

Secondly, we can invest in ourselves. By focusing on becoming stronger individuals we are, in essence, working to rewire our brains towards a positive direction. Furthermore, a stronger individual is a harder target for an abuser. Abusers naturally seek out weak individuals. They love easy prey. So, by strengthening yourself, you are investing in your own protection. Also, investing in yourself you can regain confidence and create reasons to be happy. While there is no way to change the past, who says you can't influence the future for the better? Invest in yourself by pursuing things that interests you. Seek out hobbies and pastimes that bring you joy. Look for a new job or go after a promotion. Read some books you have been putting off. In short, make your life a little more about yourself. You'll be happier and will gain some perspective, a stronger person's perspective.

Lastly, we can fill our life with loving and caring individuals. There are so many people in the world. In fact, there are enough that every each and one of us can have many loving people in our lives. Sometimes, it only takes one or two bad apples to make us think that the world is dangerous and predatory. However, if we outweigh the negative influences in our lives with positive ones, then there will be an excess of the things an abusive relationship lacks. It is among positive, caring individuals that the true value of an abusive individual makes itself known. When placed in this environment an abusive individual will stand out. And like a tumor on a MRI scan, the abusive individual will be easy to spot. Most importantly, the damage they are capable of doing will be lessened. Moving on from abusive situations becomes that much easier because now you have a loving and supportive network to help you in your healing process.

How can we move on to a happier life?

Moving on to a happier life is all about reclaiming what is rightfully yours. You have a right to be able to freely pursue your happiness. And though happiness in life is never guaranteed, you should be free from those who would actively hinder your pursuit of happiness for their own selfish or controlling reasons. People who would stand in the way of your happiness should learn to respect your personal needs and desires.

Every individual wants to have a sense of fulfillment in their life. This feeling can come from many things. Some people experience personal fulfilment by achieving goals which they have set. Accomplishing tangible goals is a great way to infuse happiness into your life. Think about some things that you have put of doing for whatever reason and set out to do them. Other people receive the greatest fulfilment by having new experiences. Traveling, trying or learning new things, and rediscovering yourself are all things you can do to encourage feelings of fulfilment. Additionally, some people may find the greatest fulfilment by initiating new friendships. As mentioned before, the positive effects of bringing in new and beneficial relationships cannot be understated. Whatever you do to pursue fulfillment, do so with unlimited conviction.

You may come to the point where you have to decide to remove individuals from your life. If this happens, stay true to your convictions. Most importantly, stay true to yourself. Realize that those who would serve to demean, lesson, or belittle you in any way, have no place in your life. Realize that you are in control of those you let into your life. You are in control. If you decide that someone's behavior in your life is abusive, or even borderline abusive, then you must stand up for yourself. You should be sure to voice your concerns and objections very clear and easy to understand language. Don't leave any room for doubt or confusion. If communicating your distaste for such behavior is unsuccessful at changing how you are treated, then the next step is to rid these people from your life.

There is no one else that can accomplish these things for you. If you want to overcome abuse and move on to a happier life, then you must be able to promise yourself that you will cultivate the resolve and believe in yourself needed to follow through with your decisions. You have to understand that you are in a position of control and authority when it comes to your life. You have all the tools and knowledge necessary to root out the abusive individuals in your life, your partner included. Keep in mind that many who display verbally abusive behavior will cease behaving in such a way when confronted. Unfortunately, some abusive individuals will not change. In cases such as these you must choose between health, happiness, and emotional well-being, or to continue experiencing verbal abuse. Ask yourself, which do you prefer?

Conclusion

Thank you again for downloading this book!

I hope this book was able to help you help you understand abusive individuals and what their presence in your life means for you. Hopefully, you were able to learn about the consequences of abuse. Also, you learned ways to manage the pain and move on to a happier life.

The next step is to follow through with your decisions. Continually reinvest in yourself and don't hesitate to take action when it comes to abuse. Remember that although you cannot control how other people behave, you can control how you respond to that behavior. You have learned to address this behavior head on and inform abusers of your power in the matter. Remember never to let anyone stand in between you and your goals, aspirations, and desires. There is no reason that you have to sacrifice these things or your sense of self-fulfillment for the sake of an abusive individual. You deserve these things.

Before you go, I'd like to say thank you for purchasing my book.
I know you could have picked so many other books to read on understanding verbal abuse. But you took a chance on me.
So A Big thanks for downloading this book and reading it all the way to completion.
Now I would like to ask a _small_ favor.

Could you please take a minute or two to leave a review for this book on Amazon?
Click here

The feedback will help me continue to publish more kindle books that will help people to get better results in their lives.
And if you found it helpful in anyway then please let me know :-)

Preview of My New Book

Body Language 101

What A Person's Body Language Is Really Telling You... And How You Can Use It To Your Advantage

Talk to the Hand

I don't know about you, but when I watch shows like *Lie to Me* or *Sherlock*, so often, I really, really wish that I could be that good. Heck, after I watched *The Mentalist* for the first time, I was studying everyone. I stared at footprints trying to see if I could tell whether the person walking was right handed or left handed. Not only is this super impractical for me as an actual skill, but it's super addicting. The thing is, it's all about studying people and watching them, but there's a science to it. I may not be out there catching criminals red handed for having a nervous tell, but it has helped me read situations and understand things that I previously missed.

So sure, you might not catch your arch-nemesis, but you might be able to understand things a little better with a little study of body language. And that's why I'm here. Body language is not just for detectives out there looking to catch murderers and thieves. Body language is the key to understanding the unspoken words that our body is communicating so heavily without our knowledge. Not only will this help you understand and relate to people better, but it'll make it so that you are aware of your own presence to others.

Nonverbal communication makes up the majority of our communication and most of us are clueless to the actual comprehension and understanding of it. That means that those who do not invest time in learning what to say in our nonverbal appearance are missing so much. But the truth is, we don't miss all of it. We have come to silently absorb and understand nonverbal communication, regardless of whether we know it or not. It's the art of learning to understand something we already know and to heighten our understanding and acceptance of what's being communicated to us. It's tricky, I know, but it's not impossible to understand.

What I'm going to tell you in this book is going to make sense to you and a lot of it is going to feel familiar, like you already knew that. Well, the reason for that is that you you've been picking up these silent transmissions for years, you just haven't acknowledged them or put a name to some of the habits you've already taught yourself.

So stick around and start to see if you can't agree or relate to some of the information you're going to receive. But more importantly, I want to address your homework before we start getting into the gritty, deep stuff. For instance, I want you to start watching people around you.

Observation is the birth of understanding and without a true sense of observance or a keen eye for noticing the little things, you're not going to pick up on some of these traits. When someone is talking to you, you're going to need to start watching them. Notice how they're standing, note the posture, have you looked at their eyes, what about the overall harmony of their face, and what are they doing with their hands? All of these things need to be running through your mind to really catch what is being conveyed to you. But not just watching their body, note the tones they're using, and the words that they're selecting. These are all going to tell you what sort of body language comes with certain attitudes and emotions. It all ties together and it is all relevant when it comes to understanding body language. So start opening your eyes and let's have a look at what they're trying to say to you.

Are you ready?

Weapons of Mass Induction

Though Sherlock Holmes often touts his use of deductive reasoning, it is actually the opposite that we're going to focus on with you, because right now, you're a student. For those of you that do not know, inductive reasoning starts with observations that slowly build a pattern that you will then form into a hypothesis until it is proven right or wrong. If you're right, then you have a theory.

For example, Kayla touches her hair a lot when she talks to Hot Mike, but not when she's talking to anyone else. So, every time I see Kayla talking to Hot Mike and she's touching her hair, that might be a cue that she likes Hot Mike. So, until I'm proven wrong, I'm certain that I have a theory that when a woman likes a man, she'll touch her hair unconsciously.

Viola, you have just jumped from observation to theory until proven wrong. Of course, when you're Sherlock Holmes level, you'll be using the art of deductive reasoning which starts at a theory and then tested with a hypothesis and observations until you have a conclusion. I think it's time for another example to prove this one to you.

[Click Here To Read The Rest of](#)

[Body Language 101](#)

[What A Person's Body Language Is Really Telling You... And How You Can Use It To Your Advantage](#)

P.S. You'll find many more books like this and others under my name Michele Gilbert.

Don't miss them... here is a short list.

Wicca: The Ultimate Beginners Guide For Witches and Warlocks: Learn Wicca Magic

The Introvert's Advantage: The Introverts Guide To Succeeding In An Extrovert World

Stop Playing Mind Games: How To Free Yourself Of Controlling And Manipulating Relationships

Instant Charisma: A Quick And Easy Guide To Talk, Impress, And Make Anyone Like You

Chakras: Understanding The 7 Main Chakras For Beginners: The Ultimate Guide To Chakra Mindfulness, Balance and Healing

Practicing Mindfulness: Living in the moment through Meditation: Everyday Habits and Rituals to help you achieve inner peace

Adrenal Fatigue: What Is Adrenal Fatigue Syndrome And How To Reset Your Diet And Your Life

Sleep Tight: Overcome Insomnia and Sleep Disorders for a better more restful sleep!

Stop Back Pain Now!: Back Pain Remedies and Treatments so you can live a pain free life!

The Arthritis Pain Cure: How to find Arthritis Pain Relief and live a happy pain free life!

The Headache Pain Cure: How to find Headache Pain Relief and live a happy Pain Free Life!

Stop Panic Attacks and Anxiety Disorders without Drugs Now!: Overcome Panic, Stress and Anxiety and live a happy pain free life!

The Breakup Recovery Guide: Advice for Surviving Heartbreak, Letting Go and Thriving in an exciting new life!

The Friendship Guide to Finding Friends Forever: How to Find, Make and Keep Quality Friendships After your Breakup

How To Stop Being Jealous And Insecure: Overcome Insecurity And Relationship Jealousy

Psychic Development: Your Guide To Unlocking Your Psychic Abilities

So I Am Dating A Psychopath: Now What?

The Mind Of A Sociopath: Your Guide to Understanding The Anti-Social Personality Disorder of Sociopaths

About Michele Gilbert

Michele Gilbert was born and raised in Brooklyn, New York. Drawn to literature and writing at a young age, she enrolled at Brooklyn College and majored in English. After graduation Michele did not begin writing immediately, instead she embarked on a career in the finance industry and spent the next thirty years on Wall Street.

Serendipity struck when she least expected it. After ending a long-term relationship, Michele found herself lost and unsure what the future held. She began to read books on grief and loss, looking for answers. Those led her to delve deeper into the Law of Attraction and its power. What resulted was remarkable. Not only had she begun to heal, she had also rekindled her former love of writing and discovered her life's purpose.

The years have taken her through many twists and turns, but she learned valuable lessons along the way. Today she publishes books-mostly self-help and metaphysical in nature-and feels compelled to share her knowledge with those facing similar experiences. Her greatest hope is to inspire others and show them ways to overcome adversity and gracefully accept life's inevitable low points.

Going forward, she plans to incorporate more teachings of self-help, finance and meditation. Regular meditation is very beneficial to her progress as she forges a new life. Morning rituals and positive incantations are other practices Michele embraces; they are very restorative in daily life.

As an avid hiker, Michele and fellow club members often hike the picturesque Jersey Pine Barrens. She is a history buff, voracious reader, baseball fanatic and a foodie. She also proudly supports Trout Unlimited-a national non-profit organization dedicated to conserving, protecting and restoring North America's Coldwater fisheries and their watersheds.

Michele currently resides forty minutes from Atlantic City and the Jersey Shore. She makes her home with a Blue Russian rescue cat named Jersey, though she isn't exactly sure who rescued who.

Michele really enjoys publishing books that can make a difference in people's lives. If you have any suggestions or would like to have a specific topic covered in a future book, please send an email to michelegilbertbooks@gmail.com and we will get back to you.

Thanks for reading!

Made in the USA
Middletown, DE
08 February 2018